Big Book of Aussie Dinosaurs

Loads of amazing prehistoric facts and hilarious pictures

Kel Richards

Illustrated by Glen Singleton

ATTACK!

The word dinosaur means 'terrible lizard'. And some Aussie dinosaurs were so terrible they would have been quite happy to eat you for breakfast!

Allosaurus was a nasty meat-eating dinosaur. She was a powerful hunter, with **sharp teeth** and three strong **claws** on each hand for attacking and holding her prey. Allosaurus could grow to be as big as a bus!

Banjo was smaller than an Allosaurus, but he was much faster and just as **scary**! Banjo had powerful back legs to run **fast** and attack any other dinosaur he decided to eat for dinner.

BIGGEST...

Dinosaurs were the largest animals to have ever lived. Some were as big as fifteen elephants and as strong as bulldozers!

George and Cooper were the biggest Aussie dinosaurs. They both had long necks and only ate plants. Just one leg bone from Cooper measured one-and-a-half metres long. That means he would have been **longer** than a railway carriage, and **heavier** than thirty cars!

...AND SMALLEST

Some dinosaurs were as small as dogs or cats—but they wouldn't have made very good pets. Even small dinosaurs could have very sharp teeth!

Skartopus is one of the smallest dinosaurs you'll meet in this book. He was a fast, meat-eating dinosaur, but was only about the size of a **chicken**! We know about this dinosaur from **tiny footprints** left in the mud millions of years ago.

DINNERTIME!

Perhaps the best-known dinosaurs are the meat-eating dinosaurs! Meat eaters are called carnivores.

> **Kakuru** wasn't very big, but he would have thought you looked good enough to **eat**! Kakuru had two long, skinny legs so he could run fast—to **catch** his dinner!

Other dinosaurs only ate plants. Plant-eating dinosaurs are called herbivores. And some dinosaurs, called omnivores, ate both meat and plants.

Clancy could grow up to fifteen metres long and three metres high—about the size of a **big whale**. Clancy could eat more than fifty kilograms of plants and leaves every day! He used his **long neck** to reach the high treetops.

DEFENCE!

Not all dinosaurs had big claws and sharp teeth, or could run very fast. Some dinosaurs had other clever ways to protect themselves against danger.

Minmi had armour of bony plates and spines over her body—she even had **spikes** on her tail. This would have made it much harder for other dinosaurs to turn her into dinner! Nasty meat-eating dinosaurs probably thought, *'I'll look for a softer dinosaur to eat!'*

Matilda may have been a gentle giant, but she was also built for defence! Matilda was so **big** that only a pack of the fiercest attacking dinosaurs were a danger. Some big dinosaurs could also use their long, strong tails to **whip** away dinosaurs who tried to attack.

SLOWEST...

Some dinosaurs could run very fast—as quick as a dog when it's chasing a cat! But some were very slow—as slow as a tortoise.

Rhoetosaurus was about as long as a house, so he wasn't built for speed! His short, stumpy legs were designed to hold his **heavy** body, not move quickly. His **top speed** was probably about the same as you walking fast, but not running.

SOUND...

Dinosaurs needed to use their eyes, ears and noses to find food to eat—and to keep out of the way of other dinosaurs!

Hadrosaur was a **noisy**, plant-eating dinosaur with a wide, flat mouth. Because of the unusual shape of his skull, he could probably make loud **hooting** and **honking** noises.

SIGHT...

Leaellynasaura was a small dinosaur with great **big eyes**. Her good eyesight helped her to see in the **dim**, cold forests of ancient Australia, and to find leaves and bushes for breakfast.

...AND SMELL!

Muttaburrasaurus also had an **unusual skull** with tubes and spaces, probably to blow out air and make loud noises, to warn his friends of danger! Muttaburrasaurus had a big, round **snout**, and a very good sense of smell.

OLDEST...

The time when dinosaurs lived, millions and millions of years ago, has been divided into three great ages—the Triassic Age, Jurassic Age and Cretaceous Age.

Ozraptor was a small, meat-eating dinosaur from the Jurassic Age. She is the **oldest known** Australian dinosaur—and would be around **175 million years** old! Ozraptor was probably a very fast hunter who fed mainly on lizards and other little animals.

...AND YOUNGEST

Wintonopus lived during the Cretaceous Age. He was a small dinosaur that ran on two legs. A herd of these dinosaurs left **tracks** in the mud—scientists think these footprints were made about **95 million years** ago. This would make Wintonopus one of Australia's youngest dinosaurs.

UP ABOVE AND DOWN BELOW

While the dinosaurs stomped and chomped and crashed and clawed their way across Australia, there were some very strange creatures living in the oceans and flying across the sky.

Nanantius was a **tiny** bird flying over the heads of the Aussie dinosaurs. She had feathers and was about the size of a **budgie**.

Pterosaurs were a type of **flying reptile** with wide wings. Some were as little as a pigeon, but others grew as large as a small **aeroplane**.

Ichthyosaurs were giant reptiles that lived in the water at the same time that the dinosaurs lived on the land. Ichthyosaurs were very **fast swimmers** and looked a bit like **dolphins**.

Kronosaurus was a gigantic underwater carnivore, and was the most **ferocious hunter** in the ocean. She had lots of huge, sharp, pointed **teeth**. She was so big that each tooth was the size of a banana!

HUNTERS...

Some kinds of dinosaurs lived in big groups called herds. They stuck together for protection, or to help each other find food. Other greedy dinosaurs liked to hunt on their own!

Tyrannosauropus was a big, meat-eating Aussie **hunter**! He left footprints in the mud, which showed three large claw-like toes. Those muddy tracks are now rock and scientists think the big Tyrannosauropus was **chasing** a herd of small dinosaurs who ran away in a stampede!

...AND HERDS

Qantassaurus was a very small plant-eating dinosaur, who probably travelled in a big group for **protection** from hungry meat eaters. It was much colder in the south of Australia than it is today, so Qantassaurus may have **burrowed** underground to hide and keep warm.

WHERE DID THEY GO?

Dinosaurs lived in Australia more than 175 million years ago. That's more years ago than you can probably imagine— and more years than you can count!

There are no dinosaurs in the world today. They all died out around 65 million years ago. When a type of animal is not alive anymore, we say it is **extinct**. No-one really knows for sure how dinosaurs became extinct.

HOW DO WE KNOW?

We know about dinosaurs from their fossils. The scientists who look for fossils and try to understand dinosaurs are called palaeontologists.

Fossils preserved in rock can show the shape of an animal or plant, or **footprints** from long, long ago. Some fossils show us what dinosaur **bones** were like. Scientists can work out what the whole dinosaur would have looked like from just a few fossils.

Aussie Dinosaur Gallery

All the dinosaurs in this book have interesting names that mean all different things. Lots of Aussie dinosaurs have been given nicknames too. Maybe that's because their proper names are very hard to say!

Allosaurus (al-uh-sore-us)

Meaning: Other lizard

Banjo is an Australovenator (oss-tra-low-ven-ah-tor)

Meaning: Southern hunter

Matilda is called Diamantinasaurus matildae (dye-ah-man-teen-ah-sore-us mah-til-day)

Meaning: Named after the Diamantina River in Queensland, and the song *Waltzing Matilda*

Hadrosaur (had-row-sore)

Meaning: Bulky lizard

Ichthyosaur (ick-thee-oh-sore)

Meaning: Fish lizard

Kakuru (ka-koo-roo)

Meaning: Aboriginal word meaning 'Rainbow Serpent'

Kronosaurus (crow-no-sore-us)

Meaning: Kronos lizard

Leaellynasaura (lee-el-in-a-sore-ah)

Meaning: Leaellyn's lizard

Minmi's full name is Minmi paravertebra (min-mee par-ah-ver-te-brah)

Meaning: Named after Minmi Crossing, near where her fossil was discovered

Muttaburrasaurus (mutt-ah-bur-rah-sore-us)

Meaning: Muttaburra lizard, named after Muttaburra in Queensland

Nanantius (nah-nan-tee-us)

Meaning: Dwarf opposite bird

Ozraptor (oz-rap-tor)

Meaning: Australian thief

Pterosaur (ter-oh-sore)

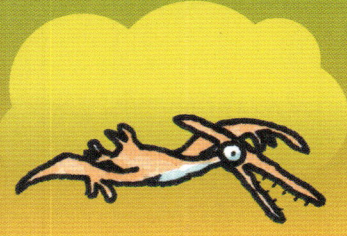

Meaning: Winged lizard

Qantassaurus (kwon-tass-sore-us)

Meaning: Qantas lizard, named after the Australian airline

Rhoetosaurus (ree-toe-sore-us)

Meaning: Trojan lizard

Skartopus (skart-oh-pus)

Meaning: Nimble foot

Timimus (tih-my-mus)

Meaning: Tim's mimic

George and Cooper are Titanosaurs (tye-tan-ah-sores)

Meaning: Titanic lizard

Tyrannosauropus (tye-ran-oh-sore-oh-pus)

Meaning: Foot of tyrant

Wintonopus (win-ton-oh-pus)

Meaning: Foot of Winton

Clancy's name is Wintonotitan (win-ton-oh-tie-tan)

Meaning: Winton giant

For William, my grandson – and for Samuel, Isabel and Joseph —KR

To Marcus Bean . . . and for Tiffany M of course! —GS

Scholastic Australia
345 Pacific Highway Lindfield NSW 2070
An imprint of Scholastic Australia Pty Limited
PO Box 579 Gosford NSW 2250
ABN 11 000 614 577
www.scholastic.com.au

Part of the Scholastic Group
Sydney • Auckland • New York • Toronto • London • Mexico City
• New Delhi • Hong Kong • Buenos Aires • Puerto Rico

First published by Scholastic Australia in 2014.
This edition published in 2015.
Text copyright © Beacon Communications, 2014.
Illustrations copyright © Glen Singleton, 2014.

All rights reserved. No part of this publication may be reproduced or transmitted in any form or by any means, electronic or mechanical, including photocopying, recording, storage in an information retrieval system, or otherwise, without the prior written permission of the publisher, unless specifically permitted under the Australian Copyright Act 1968 as amended.

National Library of Australia Cataloguing-in-Publication entry
Author: Richards, Kel, 1946- author.
Title: Big book of Aussie dinosaurs / Kel Richards; illustrated by Glen Singleton.
ISBN: 9781743626368 (paperback)
Target Audience: For primary school age.
Subjects: Dinosaurs--Australia--Juvenile literature.
Dinosaurs--Australia--Pictorial works.
Other Authors/Contributors: Singleton, Glen, 1959-, illustrator.

Typeset in Avenir and Chowderhead.

Printed in Malaysia by Tien Wah Press.

Scholastic Australia's policy, in association with Tien Wah Press, is to use papers that are renewable and made efficiently from wood grown in responsibly managed forests, so as to minimise its environmental footprint.

10 9 8 7 6 5 4 3 2 1   15 16 17 18 19 / 1